NO KNOWING

by Alan Ayckbourn

|| SAMUEL FRENCH ||

ISBN 978-0-573-11668-1

concordtheatricals.co.uk
concordtheatricals.com

FOR AMATEUR PRODUCTION ENQUIRIES

UNITED KINGDOM AND WORLD
EXCLUDING NORTH AMERICA
licensing@concordtheatricals.co.uk
020-7054-7200

Each title is subject to availability from Concord Theatricals, depending upon country of performance.

MUSIC USE NOTE

Licensees are solely responsible for obtaining formal written permission from copyright owners to use copyrighted music in the performance of this play and are strongly cautioned to do so. If no such permission is obtained by the licensee, then the licensee must use only original music that the licensee owns and controls. Licensees are solely responsible and liable for all music clearances and shall indemnify the copyright owners of the play(s) and their licensing agent, Concord Theatricals, against any costs, expenses, losses and liabilities arising from the use of music by licensees. Please contact the appropriate music licensing authority in your territory for the rights to any incidental music.

USE OF COPYRIGHT MUSIC

A licence issued by Samuel French Ltd to perform this play does not include permission to use the incidental music specified in this copy. Where the place of performance is already licensed by the PERFORMING RIGHT SOCIETY (PRS) a return of the music used must be made to them. If the place of performance is not so licensed then application should be made to the PRS, 2 Pancras Square, London, N1C 4AG (www.prsformusic.com). A separate and additional licence from PHONOGRAPHIC PERFORMANCE LTD, 1 Upper James Street, London W1F 9DE (www.ppluk.com) is needed whenever commercial recordings are used.

IMPORTANT BILLING AND CREDIT REQUIREMENTS

If you have obtained performance rights to this title, please refer to your licensing agreement for important billing and credit requirements.

NO KNOWING

First performed at the Stephen Joseph Theatre, Scarborough, in the McCarthy auditorium on 6 December 2016, with the following cast:

ARTHUR THROKE	Russell Dixon
ELSPETH THROKE	Jacqueline King
ALISON THROKE-DAVIES	Laura Matthews
NIGEL THROKE	Bill Champion

Director Alan Ayckbourn
Designer Kevin Jenkins
Lighting Mark "Tigger" Johnson

CHARACTERS

ARTHUR THROKE – a retired council official, sixties
ELSPETH THROKE – his wife, late fifties
ALISON THROKE-DAVIES – their daughter, early thirties
NIGEL THROKE – their son, late thirties

SETTING

The Throkes' semi-detached suburban family home.

PART ONE

KNOWING HER

August. The front room of the Throkes' semi-detached suburban home. It is Arthur and Elspeth's fortieth wedding anniversary. An informal gathering of family and friends.

As the lights come up, a burst of chatter. **ARTHUR,** *a man in his sixties, is standing with his two offspring,* **NIGEL** *and* **ALISON,** *both in their thirties. All of them are holding glasses. In a moment,* **NIGEL** *hits his glass with his pen. The chatter dies down.* **ARTHUR** *steps forward.*

ARTHUR Ladies and gentlemen, thank you, all of you, for coming out today to help Elspeth and me to celebrate our forty years. Whilst it's our celebration, we want you all, friends, neighbours, family to enjoy yourselves and to have a really good time. Before I start, we'd like, both of us, to give special thanks to our son and daughter, Alison and Nigel, for laying on this surprise for us. Even though me and Elspeth have known about it for ages. You can't keep a secret for long, not in our family. But I can't let this moment pass without saying a few words about my wonderful wife, over there. As her husband and junior partner, I think it's fair to say, although you're all of you close family or friends, that I probably know her better than most of you. So anyway, here goes...

He pauses to retrieve some crumpled notes from his inside pocket and puts on his reading glasses. **NIGEL** *and* **ALISON** *seat themselves behind him, at first respectfully listening, but as* **ARTHUR** *proceeds with his oration, barely concealing their incredulity.*

(having finally got himself sorted) You know, it's been said marriage is a funny thing. You start off making a lifetime promise to someone you barely know – well you *think* you

know them, of course you do, but then at that age you think you know everything, don't you? But of course you don't. You can't possibly. I mean. After all, what was I? Twenty-three? How could I know everything there was to know about anyone at twenty-three? Specially not a woman! But there I was, promising my life away to a virtual stranger. Let's face it, at twenty-three, I barely knew myself. Mind you, that's not to say I didn't love her. Of course, I was in love with her. I was mad about the girl. I felt I couldn't live without her. But, if I'm honest, I knew bugger all about her. And she barely knew me. But as the years passed, we grew into each other, as it were. Till we were like a couple of pot plants. Couple of busy Lizzies. Couldn't tell where one of us started and the other one finished. How do they put it? Inseparably entwined. As years went by, we both faced life as one. And between us we saw it off together. While I was up there slaving away at the town hall, Ellie's been back here. Keeping things straight. Making sure these two grew up good and strong with the right values.

And I'm proud to say – between us, Ellie and me, we didn't do a bad job, did we?

He briefly favours **NIGEL** *and* **ALISON** *with a smile.*

Well, the years have rolled by, water's flown under the bridge and we're still here. Clinging on for dear life. I think it's only right to take this occasion publicly to say thank you to her. In public. I've said it plenty of times to her in private, but in public. Thank you, Ellie, for forty years. Forty years of love, comradeship and friendship. I'm not saying we haven't had our moments. There were days, specially early on, when the kitchen china was flying about. Days when I did well to keep me head down. But, as I say, that was the early days. Later on, we both got things into proportion, once we got to know each other better, we learnt to sense each other's needs. To sense the times when we needed to be there for each other – and, just as important, the times when we needed to keep our distance. Allow each other space to breathe. We grew to sense that. In the end it became – symbiosis – yes, yes, I had to look that up as well – for your information, George, "symbiosis – meaning 'interaction between two different organisms'" – no, organisms, Janice, not what you're thinking, woman – Jeff, control your wife please – "meaning 'interaction between two different *organisms* living in close physical association, especially to the advantage of both.'" Which, when you think about it, sums it all up really, marriage. She's a wonderful woman and dare I say it, a perfect wife. To have known Ellie is to love her. To have known her as well as I do, makes me the proudest, most privileged man in the world. Ladies and gentlemen, may I give you the toast, to Elspeth, Jane, Elizabeth, my lovely, loving wife, thank you and God bless you!

OTHERS *(variously)* To Elspeth! Ellie!

They raise their glasses and toast.

The lights fade, briefly.

Party music and a burst of chatter as the gathering resumes.

The lights come up on the kitchen. Two doors, the back door and one to the rest of the house and the front door.

It is two weeks before Christmas of the previous year.

ARTHUR *is sitting at the table, finishing his tea.* **ELSPETH** *is pottering round him, starting to clear away.*

ARTHUR Very nice.

ELSPETH Yes, it was nice. Very nice.

ARTHUR Very nice indeed. Tasty.

---

*A licence to produce *No Knowing* does not include a performance licence for any third-party or copyrighted music. Licensees should create an original composition or use music in the public domain. For further information, please see Music Use Note on page iii.

ELSPETH Yes it was, tasty. I might go there again. He has good meat, that man.

ARTHUR He knows his meat.

ELSPETH He does.

ARTHUR What man's that?

ELSPETH The new one. You know, on the far corner. Used to be Wicksteed's.

ARTHUR Wicksteed's?

ELSPETH Wicksteed's. That deli that came and went.

ARTHUR I don't remember that. I don't remember there being a deli.

ELSPETH It was only there three months. Less than that. Before that it was Gravewood's.

ARTHUR Gravewood's.

ELSPETH Luggage.

ARTHUR Luggage?

ELSPETH Leather goods and luggage.

ARTHUR Oh, that place. Gravewood's. Did that close, then?

ELSPETH Been closed for over a year. Until it became Wicksteed's. Now it's this new butcher's. Cattershaw's.

ARTHUR Well, there you go. Everything changes given time. Most of it for the worse.

ELSPETH Right.

A pause.

Mind you, it was never a pleasant shop, was Gravewood's. I never liked it. They weren't a particularly nice couple. He was offhand and she was downright rude, most of the time. Very overpriced, too, their luggage. I never went in there at all, not if I could avoid it.

ARTHUR I never did go in. Never bought anything in Gravewood's. Not a single suitcase.

ELSPETH What would you be doing, buying a suitcase? You never go anywhere.

A pause.

Still. He's a good butcher, this Mr Cattershaw, I'll say that for him. We're long overdue for a good butcher's round here, aren't we?

ARTHUR He certainly knows his meat.

ELSPETH Time will tell.

ARTHUR So far, so good. *(making to rise from the table)* Well...

ELSPETH Had enough, have you?

ARTHUR Yes, I'd better get back.

ELSPETH Back to your shed?

ARTHUR Just for a moment or two.

ELSPETH Moment or two? Come on, you'll be in there for hours –

ARTHUR No, I won't –

ELSPETH You always are. On that computer. Hours on end. God knows what you get up to.

ARTHUR I tell you, once you get on to the Internet, Ellie, you've got the world at your feet. At your command. Whatever you want to know. Whatever you need to see. Wherever you want to go. No need for suitcases.

ELSPETH Not the same though, is it? As going there?

ARTHUR Far cheaper. Quicker, too. Don't like the look of a place, press a button, back you come.

ELSPETH *(unconvinced)* Well, each to his own.

ARTHUR *hovers by the back door.*

I'll be out for a couple of hours.

ARTHUR *(uninterested)* Oh yes?

ELSPETH I'm meeting up with Janice.

ARTHUR Oh, yes?

ELSPETH Just for a chat. Perhaps have a drink.

ARTHUR I don't know. Gallivanting around.

ELSPETH I'd hardly call sitting in Trudy's Wine Bar with half a glass of Chardonnay, gallivanting. She needs to get out, poor woman. Her husband's worse than you are. Sitting in front of a screen for hours.

ARTHUR What, Jeff? I didn't know that. On the Internet?

ELSPETH No, he watches videos, never stops. Morning, noon and night.

ARTHUR Why can't he and Janice watch them together?

ELSPETH He only watches westerns. John Wayne movies. Over and over again. Round and round. Knows them all by heart. Janice says he sits there with the sound turned down, muttering the dialogue under his breath. What sort of evening's that for her, poor woman? Night after night?

ARTHUR Ah, well. Each to his own. *(restlessly, anxious to leave)* Well...

ELSPETH Yes. Look at the time. I must change. I'll be late for her, otherwise... See you later.

ARTHUR Right. See you later.

ELSPETH *goes into the hall.*

ARTHUR *is about to leave through the back door when, after a moment, the front doorbell chimes.*

ELSPETH *(off, calling)* Arthur, could you see who that is?

ARTHUR I'll go!

He goes off to the hall.

(offstage) Hallo, Nigel, what brings you round here?

He returns, followed by **NIGEL** *in his coat.*

Didn't know we were expecting you. Nice surprise.

NIGEL No, I just wanted a word, Dad. You know, a private word. I thought you might be, you know, out in your shed. Where you usually are, you know.

ARTHUR Yes, I was on my way out there. Only just finished my tea.

NIGEL Ah, right.

ARTHUR Get back on the computer.

NIGEL Still trawling, then, are you?

ARTHUR Still trawling. Amazing what you find. Amazing what's out there.

NIGEL Yes. Amazing.

ARTHUR Nothing like that when I was young. Had to go to the library, if you wanted to find out anything. Then they usually hadn't got it.

NIGEL Still using my old laptop, then?

ARTHUR Oh, yes.

NIGEL Surprised it's still going.

ARTHUR Oh, yes, it's still going. Bit slow now, by modern standards I expect. Creaks and groans a bit. But it does the job...

NIGEL So long as it can still find the porn sites, eh?

ARTHUR Sorry?

NIGEL Sorry.

ARTHUR I'm having none of that. None of that, if you don't mind, son. I wiped all that filth. The day after I got it, young man, the day after you gave it to me.

NIGEL Wiped all what?

ARTHUR You know. Don't worry I saw them. Amongst your list
of "Personal Favourites." Be ashamed of yourself.

NIGEL Well, I was only young, you know...

ARTHUR Old enough to know better. *Pussies in Boots*, indeed!
Could have had the police round. Son of mine. Didn't catch
your sister looking at things like that, did we?

NIGEL What, Alison? She introduced me to them...she...

He trails off.

ARTHUR What?

NIGEL Nothing.

A pause. NIGEL *seems uneasy.*

ARTHUR Your mother's upstairs.

NIGEL Ah.

ARTHUR She's on her way out. She's getting changed. She'll be
down in a minute.

NIGEL Right.

A slight pause.

Maybe this isn't a good time, then? You know...

ARTHUR A good time for what?

NIGEL For – for us to have a chat. A private chat. You know.

ARTHUR Oh, I see. Private.

Another slight pause.

Want to take your coat off, then?

NIGEL Oh, yes, right. *(taking off his coat)* Might as well. If
we're planning to stop in here, you know. Might as well. Yes.

ARTHUR We can go in the front room, if you'd rather. If it's
going to be that private?

NIGEL No, here's fine. Here's fine.

ARTHUR Only there's no heating on in there. We won't be switching that on till Christmas Eve. There's no point. Here, let me take that for you.

NIGEL No, it's all right, Dad, I can –

ARTHUR No, no, I'll do it, I can do it. You sit down.

He goes out momentarily.

NIGEL *looks around anxiously.*

(offstage, calling) It's Nigel, love...

ELSPETH *(offstage, calling)* Who?

ARTHUR *(offstage, calling)* Nigel. He's just popped in for a word.

ELSPETH *(offstage, calling)* Oh, lovely. Tell him I'll be down in a minute.

ARTHUR *returns.*

NIGEL *sits.*

ARTHUR *(confidentially)* She'll be down in a minute. Now, what was it you wanted to talk to me about? Something private, you say?

NIGEL Yes, it was...

ARTHUR Was it to do with Christmas? Were you going to ask me what your mother wants for Christmas –?

NIGEL What? Oh, no...

ARTHUR – I bet that's what it is, isn't it –?

NIGEL No, no...

ARTHUR No, it'll be the usual, for both of us. Tokens. Can't go wrong with tokens. You know your mother, always wants the same things, every birthday, every Christmas. I always give her the same. Toiletries. Ever since we were first married, I've always given her toiletries. Till about ten years ago, then after that, it was tokens. So she could choose her own. Toiletry tokens. She's always been perfectly content with toiletries –

NIGEL No, Dad, that's not what I wanted to talk –

ARTHUR As for me, Amazon tokens. Can't go far wrong with Amazon tokens, can you? Or possibly IKEA.

NIGEL Dad – *(rising)* Do you mind if I shut the door a minute?

ARTHUR No. You in a draught, then?

NIGEL *closes the door.*

NIGEL It's not about Christmas. It's about Mum.

ARTHUR What about her?

NIGEL It's – er... Oh, bloody hell, I don't know where to start with this, I really don't... It's difficult, you know...

A pause.

ARTHUR How's Denise keeping, then? Bearing up, is she?

NIGEL Oh, yes. She's – bearing up. She's well.

ARTHUR *(laughing)* Won't be too long before she's bearing down, will it? Eh?

NIGEL *(smiling faintly)* No, not so long now...

ARTHUR Seven months, isn't she? Bet she's crossing off the days, eh?

NIGEL *(smiling faintly)* Yes.

ARTHUR Bet you both are. Never mind, not long now. Next time you turn round he'll be a teenager.

NIGEL Yes, I suppose –

ARTHUR Are you excited, both of you? You must be excited, being your first?

NIGEL Yes, we're very excited.

ARTHUR Not before time, lad. Shame on you, letting Alison beat you to it. Your sister beat you to it by two years, what were you thinking? She and her Brian. At it like rabbits.

NIGEL Well, you know, Denise – She didn't really feel she was ready...

ARTHUR Ready? Of course she was ready.

NIGEL Well, no, it was –

ARTHUR What'd she get married for, if she wasn't ready?

NIGEL No, it's not –

ARTHUR What else does a woman get married for? To have kids. That's what women get married for. No reason to get married otherwise. Not necessarily why men get married, but it's the only reason a woman gets married. Unless he has to. Woman gets married to have children. Man gets married 'cause he has to have 'em.

NIGEL It's different these days, Dad. Women have other reasons for marrying – they have, you know, different – parameters...

ARTHUR Rubbish. Parameters! Woman's a woman. Man's a man. Fact of nature. Always has been, always will be.

NIGEL Not these days. These days, that's all changed – Denise still isn't certain, you know. She's still not really sure she wants to go through with it. "You're sure we're doing the right thing," she keeps saying. "Bringing a child into a world like this?"

ARTHUR I'll tell you something, Nigel. My grandmother on my mother's side, she had nine children. Nine in total! Lost two in childbirth, lost another aged five from TB, brought four survivors up, virtually single-handed, while my grandfather was away in the trenches fighting for his life. He came home, one leg missing, they promptly went and had two more of them! And I can tell you, God rest her soul, she died a happy, satisfied woman.

NIGEL She probably had no choice.

ARTHUR Anyway, you're not to worry about Denise. It's natural. It's an ordeal for a woman. She's apprehensive, it's her first. By the time she's had a couple more, she'll be laughing. Now what did you want to talk about? She'll be down in a minute.

NIGEL Yes, well, I don't know how to put this. Mum's been behaving – slightly inappropriately, you know...

ARTHUR How do you mean, inappropriately? What's inappropriately?

NIGEL Well, I ran into Jeff, you know, Jeff Thorpe at work yesterday. In the staff canteen. Jeff Thorpe from accounts, lives on the estate here, you know.

ARTHUR Yes, I know Jeff. Number eighteen. Married to Janice, isn't he? I forgot he worked with you –

NIGEL Well, normally I don't see much of him, me being down there in maintenance, whilst he's up there in accounts, you know. But we just happened to run into each other, just by chance and we got talking and suddenly he poured it all out to me. It's apparently the talk of this estate – you're probably the only one who doesn't know –

ARTHUR Know what? What don't I know?

NIGEL You know this estate, what it's like. What did we used to say when we were kids growing up here? Break wind at number twelve and they're fanning themselves at number sixty-five. There's no secrets around here. Not for long. All the time we were growing up, you know, Ali and me, we couldn't wait to get away from the place.

ARTHUR So what exactly are we talking about? What's this thing everyone knows except me?

NIGEL Well, it appears, you know, rumour has it, that Mum and Mrs Thorpe are conducting, you know, a relationship. You know.

ARTHUR A relationship?

NIGEL Apparently?

ARTHUR Your mother?

NIGEL So it's said.

ARTHUR With Mrs – with Janice Thorpe?

NIGEL I know it's hard to credit.

ARTHUR Well, they're friends, aren't they? Good friends?

NIGEL They're more than that. They were seen by someone. You know. Kissing –

ARTHUR Kissing?

NIGEL Passionately. Apparently.

ARTHUR Where? Where were they kissing?

NIGEL On the mouth.

ARTHUR No, where? Where? What was the location? Their geographical location?

NIGEL The bus shelter on the corner of Hoxton Road. Holding each other, you know, close. You know. Tightly.

ARTHUR Well – that doesn't – that was – they were probably trying to keep warm. It gets very draughty on that corner.

NIGEL They were also seen in that wine bar. Trudy's. Fiddling under the table. You know.

ARTHUR Fiddling? What sort of fiddling?

NIGEL You know. Fiddling. With each other.

ARTHUR Well, that's women, isn't it? That's just women being – women. They're forever touching each other and titifillating. That doesn't mean anything. They're not like us men, are they? We don't sit there fiddling with each other, do we? No, this is complete nonsense, it's libel – a slander. Where did Jeff get this from, for God's sake? Why hasn't he said anything before? Why's he not spoken to me? Why did he come sneaking up to you in the works canteen?

NIGEL He said, he only found out yesterday. He said he'd heard rumours but it was like you, you know, he didn't believe them. Put it down to wagging tongues and malicious gossip.

But then a couple of nights ago, Mum was apparently coming round to their house to look at some catalogues Janice had sorted out for her, Mrs Thorpe's one of those agents, you know, selling things, makeup and so on. And Jeff decided to find out for himself so he made an excuse and told her he was out for the evening. But then an hour or so later, you know, he sneaked back and found them both in bed together.

ARTHUR In bed?

NIGEL Their double. Both of them semi-naked, so far as he could tell. In each other's arms, you know.

ARTHUR Oh, my God! What did they say?

NIGEL Nothing. They were both fast asleep.

ARTHUR Asleep?

NIGEL You know. Smiling, apparently.

ARTHUR So what did he do? What did Jeff do then?

NIGEL Well, he tip-toed out again. What else could he do?

ARTHUR Probably the best thing in the circumstances.

NIGEL He went back downstairs and watched a John Wayne film.

ARTHUR *(digesting this)* I see. I see. I see.

A pause.

He considers all this.

(at length) No. This isn't right, you know.

NIGEL How do you mean, exactly, Dad? Not right? I mean, I don't think you can morally disapprove, can you, not these days. It's perfectly legal –

ARTHUR Not with my wife, it isn't –

NIGEL I mean, it's not like the old days, is it? I mean, today, you know, if two people of the same sex choose to get into bed together, you can't –

ARTHUR No, that's not what I mean. It's rubbish. It's nonsense. That's never her, that's never your mother. I've known the woman for forty years next August, for God's sake! And what's more, I have been constantly in bed with her. I sleep next to the woman every night. I'd know! That's never Elspeth, never in a million years. I know that woman back to front. Inside out. She hasn't got a bent bone in her body –

NIGEL Yes, but how would you know, Dad? How could you tell if she wasn't that way inclined? How can you?

ARTHUR I'd know. All right? That's all I can say. I'm a man. I'd know. We've – we've – done it together. You know. Done *it*. Frequently. Dozens of times. We've had two kids for God's sake! We've had you and your sister. Living proof. There you are. My case rests. I'm saying no more about it.

A slight pause.

NIGEL *(hesitantly)* I still –

ARTHUR *(angrily)* I've said that's enough, son! I don't want any more of that mucky talk. For Christ's sake, it's nearly Christmas! I mean, I've nothing against them. Don't get me wrong. That sort of thing... I'm as broad-minded as the next man. If people choose to behave – unnaturally – that's entirely up to them. I wouldn't condemn it as wrong but in my book, it's definitely downright unnatural. And I won't have that sort of filth said about your mother. End of conversation. My final word.

A long pause.

NIGEL I still think you should talk to her, Dad. You know, have it out with her. I really think you should, Dad. At least talk to Mum. Please. Both of you, have a conversation about it. After all, if she's doing this... There might be things she's – you know –

ARTHUR What? There might be things she's what –?

NIGEL You know, hiding from you? Bottling, something deeper? You know? Some sort of unhappiness?

ARTHUR She's hiding nothing from me. She couldn't possibly. Forty years, I can read her like a book. Open book to me, that woman. Always has been.

NIGEL Well, you know, it might be some time since you picked her up and read her, Dad. She might just have written herself another chapter.

ARTHUR Rubbish. Have you talked about this to your sister? Have you told Alison?

NIGEL No. I don't think Alison knows. I've not told her.

ARTHUR Well, don't say a word to her. It'd really upset her. You know how she worships your mother.

NIGEL No, I won't say a word. Mind you, it's only a matter of time till she does hear about it. Knowing this place.

ELSPETH *enters. She is now made-up and looks rather smart, almost chic.*

She immediately senses there is an atmosphere.

ELSPETH Sorry to interrupt. Were you both in the middle of something?

ARTHUR No, not at all. We were – we were just –

NIGEL – Talking about Christmas presents.

ELSPETH Oh...

NIGEL Wondering what you wanted for Christmas, Mum?

ELSPETH Oh, well...

NIGEL By the way, you're looking gorgeous. Very glamorous.

ELSPETH Oh, well, I just stuck a bit of makeup on –

NIGEL Lovely –

ELSPETH – Since I was going out. Tidied myself up a bit...

NIGEL Doesn't she, Dad?

ARTHUR Eh?

NIGEL Lovely. Doesn't Mum look lovely?

ARTHUR *(barely glancing at her)* Oh, yes. Lovely.

NIGEL Where you going, Mum? Anywhere nice?

ELSPETH No, not really. Just for a quick drink round the corner.

NIGEL On your own?

ELSPETH No, I'm meeting Janice. My friend Janice.

NIGEL Ah.

> *A silence.*

> With Janice?

ELSPETH Janice Thorpe. Married to Jeff Thorpe. You remember them, surely? Doesn't he work with you?

NIGEL Oh, yes, I remember her, now. Janice Thorpe! Nice woman. Lovely woman! She's great.

ELSPETH Yes, she's very pleasant.

NIGEL Friendly.

ELSPETH Yes, she is. She's very friendly.

NIGEL Well, it's good to have a friend, Mum. That's what I say. I mean, there's nothing like it, is there? Friendship? You know. That's what friends are for, aren't they? For friendship.

ELSPETH *(slightly puzzled)* Yes.

ARTHUR Nigel...

NIGEL Dad?

ARTHUR Leave it, lad.

NIGEL Right.

> *A slight pause.*

ELSPETH So what's all this about Christmas presents, then? You were asking me what I wanted?

ARTHUR I told him. You'll have tokens. I've said to him they're not to bother looking for anything. We'll both of us be happy with the usual tokens.

NIGEL Is that what you'd like, Mum? Tokens? Same as usual?

ARTHUR Yes, she would.

ELSPETH Well, you know, this year – this year – what I'd really like…

NIGEL Yes, what's that, Mum? What would you really like…?

ELSPETH What I'd really love is a little surprise. Something I'm not expecting, you know. Just something – different.

ARTHUR Don't ask for that, woman! You'll end up with a dartboard or a pair of roller skates.

ELSPETH They'd be fun. I've always wanted to roller skate.

ARTHUR I was joking.

ELSPETH I wasn't.

NIGEL It's all right, Mum, I'll think of something. Well, Mum, Dad, if you'll both excuse me, I have to dash. I promised Denise, I'd…

ELSPETH Oh, aren't you staying? Have a chat with your dad?

ARTHUR We've had our chat.

NIGEL No, we've had a chat, thanks. Sorry, Mum, must run. I'll leave you two to talk. You know. Why don't you two have a good talk, together? Eh, Dad?

ELSPETH Us? What on earth have we two got to talk about?

NIGEL *(leaving)* I'll see myself out. Bye.

He goes out.

The front door slams, off.

ELSPETH You all right?

ARTHUR Fine.

ELSPETH You seem a bit quiet. Quieter than normal.

Oh, I never asked after Denise. Is she all right, did he say? How's she coping?

ARTHUR She's fine.

A slight pause.

ELSPETH Nigel looks well.

ARTHUR He's fine.

A slight pause.

ELSPETH What you doing now? Going back to your shed, are you?

ARTHUR Just for an hour or two.

ELSPETH Well, I'll try not to be too late. Don't forget to lock the back door after you, will you?

ARTHUR Right.

He opens the back door, removing the key.

ELSPETH See you later, then.

ARTHUR See you later.

He goes out, locking the back door behind him.

ELSPETH *takes her mobile from her bag and speed-dials.*

ELSPETH Hallo, sweet...yes, I'm sorry, I'm just on my way, love. I got...yes...you right then, sweet? ...Yes, I'll be with you in a minute, darling. I'm just on my way now...yes...yes...and me you...yes...yes...bye...

She mouths a soft kiss.

She replaces the phone in her bag and takes a final look round the kitchen.

(to herself, with a sigh) Oh, well. Soon be Christmas, anyway...

She goes out, turning off the lights. As she does so, the lights fade to:

Blackout.

PART TWO

KNOWING HIM

August. The front room of the Throkes' semi-detached suburban home. It is Arthur and Elspeth's fortieth wedding anniversary. An informal gathering of family and friends.

As the lights come up, a burst of chatter. **ELSPETH,** *a woman in her late fifties, is standing with her two offspring,* **NIGEL** *and* **ALISON,** *both in their thirties. All of them are holding glasses. In a moment,* **NIGEL** *hits his glass with his pen. The chatter dies down.* **ELSPETH** *steps forward.*

ELSPETH Ladies and gentlemen, on behalf of us both, thank you, all of you, for coming out today, to help Arthur and me to celebrate forty years. He's asked me to speak first, I suspect only in order that he can get the last word in. Welcome, friends, neighbours, family. We want you to enjoy yourselves and, please, while you're here, have a really good time. Before I start, I'd like to say a special thanks to my son and daughter, Alison and Nigel here, for arranging all this. Thank you so much, both of you. We know how busy you both are and your dad and I really appreciate it. Since I find myself standing here in front of all of you, which was really not my choice, believe me, but my children insisted I should say something, I'd like to say a little bit about marriage, particularly from a woman's point of view, if you'll forgive me. But since I am a woman and have been for nearly sixty years and I've been married for forty of them, I do think that I qualify as being something of an expert.

She pauses to gather her thoughts. We sense that, whereas the preceding was scripted, from now on she's speaking spontaneously and with increasing confidence. **NIGEL** *and* **ALISON** *seat themselves behind her, at first respectfully*

listening, but as ELSPETH *proceeds with her speech,*
barely concealing their incredulity.

ELSPETH When I first got married, it was the accepted thing
that a young wife in those days would do all she could to
keep her new husband interested in her. Usually working
on the principle that most men are creatures of habit, by
doing her best to remain looking exactly the same year
after year for as long as possible. But I soon abandoned
that, realising that way usually left you as mutton dressed
as lamb. The alternative, but one that didn't half take it
out of you, was to keep ringing the changes, on the other
principle that men, when it comes to women, have a very
limited attention span. So I chose the second alternative
and kept frantically altering myself, week in week out, till
as I say I wore myself out. And half the time Arthur, bless
him, being a man, never even noticed, anyway. And then,
after a few years, as the children grew up, Alison, my teenage
daughter, as she was then, said to me – and really, you know,
it took a modern teenager to say it – she said, "Why do you
bother, Mum? Why not just try being yourself?" And you
know, it was just so obvious, so simple but I'd never ever
thought of it. After all, she said, "Dad never alters, does
he? He's exactly the same, year after year, ever since I was
born." And I thought to myself, yes, and before that, as
well. It came to me in a blinding flash. She was right. Why
not just be myself? After all it was myself he fell in love
with, presumably. It was myself he married. Sod him, he
was going to have to live with myself, wasn't he? So for a
lot of you out there who might possibly be contemplating
marriage – though I can see a few of you have already been
round that circuit, once or twice – take my advice and stay
true to yourself. It may not be the easiest path, it'll have
its moments, it's bound to, there'll be times when you'll be
tempted to weaken, but at the end of it at least you'll still
be yourself. I'd like you now to raise a glass to my husband
for all the years of being there when I needed him to be
but also for allowing me, now and then, the space to be
myself. To Arthur.

OTHERS *(variously)* Arthur! To Arthur!

They raise their glasses and toast.

The lights fade, briefly.

Party music and a burst of chatter as the gathering resumes.[*]

The lights come up on the kitchen. Two doors, the back door and one to the rest of the house and the front door.

It is the week before Christmas of the previous year.

ARTHUR *is sitting at the table, finishing his tea.* **ELSPETH** *is pottering round him, starting to clear away.*

ARTHUR Very nice.

ELSPETH Did you like it, then?

ARTHUR Didn't you?

ELSPETH Well, I thought it was a bit on the dry side, really.

ARTHUR Oh, yes, it was dry.

ELSPETH That's what I said.

ARTHUR What do you expect, it was fish. Fish is always dry.

ELSPETH It doesn't have to be.

ARTHUR Fish, once it's out of the water, it's dry, isn't it? That's how it is with fish.

ELSPETH Well, I prefer it more moist.

ARTHUR Raw? You prefer it raw.

ELSPETH No, not raw. Just slightly more – moist.

---

*A licence to produce *No Knowing* does not include a performance licence for any third-party or copyrighted music. Licensees should create an original composition or use music in the public domain. For further information, please see Music Use Note on page iii.

ARTHUR Batter.

ELSPETH What?

ARTHUR That's why it's usually cooked in batter. Fish. To keep in the moisture. Seals it, you see. Keeps it moist. The batter acts as seal. It seals it.

ELSPETH That wasn't cooked in batter. I didn't cook it in batter.

ARTHUR That's why it was dry. You should have cooked it in batter, if you wanted it moist.

ELSPETH Well, more fool me, wasn't I, trying something different. I knew you'd complain.

ARTHUR I'm not complaining.

ELSPETH Yes you did, you said it was dry.

ARTHUR I didn't say it was dry. You're the one who said it was dry. I never said it was dry.

ELSPETH You agreed with me, though.

ARTHUR Oh, I agreed with you but I wasn't the one who said it. You're the one who said it. You're the one who said it was dry.

ELSPETH Well, it was. I thought it was.

ARTHUR Oh, yes. I said, it was certainly dry. But then you know me, I'm never that keen on fish.

ELSPETH No, well, I certainly won't do it again.

ARTHUR Never been fond of fish. Unless it's in batter. *(making to rise from the table)* Well...

ELSPETH Had enough, have you?

ARTHUR Yes, I'd better get back.

ELSPETH Back to your shed?

ARTHUR Just for a moment or two.

ELSPETH Moment or two? Come on, you'll be in there for hours –

ARTHUR No, I won't –

ELSPETH You always are. On that computer. Hours on end. God knows what you get up to...

ARTHUR Once you get on to the Internet, Ellie, the world's your oyster. The font of all knowledge, the Internet. Whatever you want to know, it's there.

ELSPETH That's not what I've heard. Nigel says, very often –

ARTHUR In the old days, this bloke came to the door and talked my dad into putting down a deposit for a set of *Britannica*s. *Encyclopaedia Britannica*s. Thirty-two volumes, delivered month by month. My dad built a special bookshelf just for them. Over the months, we kids watched the shelves fill up, volume by volume. In the end, it weighed a bloody ton.

ELSPETH Useful, though. Thoughtful of your dad.

ARTHUR Not that we ever read 'em. Never even opened half of them.

ELSPETH What a waste.

ARTHUR We were too busy out playing football. Well...

He hovers by the back door.

ELSPETH Alison's round in a minute...

ARTHUR *(uninterested)* Oh yes?

ELSPETH Said she wanted a private word with me. Probably wants to talk about Christmas.

ARTHUR Christmas? What's there to talk about there?

ELSPETH Probably wanting to know what we both wanted.

ARTHUR Us? We're no problem, are we? Always have the same, don't we? Always the same, Alison knows that?

ELSPETH Yes, well...

ARTHUR Every Christmas, every birthday. She knows us by now, surely? We're easy enough. We're both happy with tokens, aren't we? *(anxious to leave)* I'll get on, then...

ELSPETH You're not waiting to say hallo to her?

ARTHUR No, she's coming to see you. Private word, you said. You don't want me here, do you? Give her my love. See you later.

He unlocks the back door and goes out, closing it behind him.

ELSPETH *stands undecided for a moment.*

She slowly starts to tidy away.

In a moment, the doorbell chimes.

She goes out to the hall to answer the door.

ALISON *(offstage)* Hallo, Mum! Sorry I'm a bit late...

ELSPETH *(offstage)* You're not late. Give me your coat.

ALISON *(offstage)* Traffic's terrible. It's late-night shopping.

ELSPETH *(offstage)* Yes, I know, it's all week, isn't it?

ALISON It gets crazier every year, Christmas. Spend, spend, spend.

ELSPETH *(as she re-enters)* Right. Come in, love. It's warmer in here. It's the only room that is warm. Apart from the bedroom.

ALISON *(following her in)* Why's it so cold, then? I thought you had central heating.

ELSPETH We only use it in certain rooms. Now it's just two of us...

ALISON What's the point of that? It's central, isn't it? *Central* heating, that's the whole point of it, surely?

ELSPETH You know what he's like. "I'm not paying to heat rooms if neither of us is going to be sitting in them."

ALISON He'd better warm this place up before Christmas. I'm not bringing the kids round here, they'll die of hypothermia. Brian keeps our house at boiling point.

ELSPETH Oh, he'll switch it all on before you come round. It's all right. I get used to it. You just have to keep moving. It's healthier really. Good for me.

ALISON He's turned into bloody Scrooge, Dad, hasn't he? Only heating in here and the bedroom?

ELSPETH And in his shed, of course. He's got a fan heater in there. That front room's like an icebox, there's real frost on that Christmas tree.

ALISON Yes, it looks nice from the street, the tree, through the front window. That and Rudolph on the roof.

ELSPETH Oh, yes, we have to have Rudolph on the roof, don't we? Wouldn't be Christmas without Rudolph, would it?

ALISON What do you mean, Christmas? He sits up there all year round, doesn't he? He sits there in July.

ELSPETH Well it's a big job for your dad, these days, getting him up and down again. These days, I try and keep him away from ladders. Rudolph's not switched on normally, is he? Never gets switched on till the first of December. Then, on the dot of New Year's morning off he goes again. Every year, like clockwork. You know what your dad's like for tradition.

ALISON Yes, Rudolph. Ever since I can remember.

ELSPETH Good to have traditions, though. Carols...and...crackers... and...

ALISON Reindeers on the roof.

ELSPETH Yes... Besides it's nice for the neighbours to look at.

ALISON They're the only people who can see it. We can't. Unless we stand in the middle of the road. Don't you ever consider changing it?

ELSPETH What?

ALISON Put something else up there one year for a change? Something different? Give the neighbours a treat. Something other than a reindeer?

ELSPETH What? What else is there?

ALISON I don't know. Some other sort of animal. A cat? A lion? A gorilla? King Kong?

ELSPETH Not very Christmassy. Having a gorilla on your roof. Not very suitable for Jesus' birthday, a gorilla, surely?

ALISON Neither's a reindeer, for that matter. He didn't ride into Bethlehem on a bloody reindeer, did he? That's it! A donkey! You could put a donkey up there instead, Mum. Cut Rudolph's horns off and turn him into a donkey.

ELSPETH No, we couldn't do that to Rudolph. Your dad wouldn't allow that.

ALISON Where is he, by the way? Out in his shed?

ELSPETH Yes, he sends his love. He's sorry he missed you. He's a bit busy.

ALISON On his computer?

ELSPETH God knows what he gets up to, I never ask. So long as it keeps him from under my feet...

ALISON You've no idea at all what he gets up to?

ELSPETH No.

ALISON You really haven't the faintest idea what Dad does on that computer, Mum, night after night? You've absolutely no idea?

ELSPETH Why? What are you...? Oh, he's not into something mucky, is he? You know, something nasty? Oh, Alison, I couldn't bear it if he was into something nasty?

ALISON No, it's not – no – not nasty, not like you're thinking. Not that sort of nasty –

ELSPETH He's not been – breaking the law, has he? He hasn't been intercepted by the police or anything?

ALISON No, nothing like –

ELSPETH I mean, I've read about it, they send these unmarked vans round with detectors and they intercept the signals –

ALISON I think that's for TV licences, Mum –

ELSPETH No, that's the way they catch them these days, Alison, catch them watching illegal things. I'd hate it if I thought your dad was watching illegal things, that'd be terrible –

ALISON No, Mum, it's nothing illegal – well I think maybe technically it is illegal – but Dad's not doing anything like that. Not like you're imagining.

ELSPETH But it is against the law, you say? What he's doing is breaking the law?

ALISON I think, technically, it might be, yes.

ELSPETH Oh, dear, that's terrible. I thought the worst he was up to was maybe looking at a few pictures, occasionally. Those sort of pictures, you know. Naturist pictures, we used to call them. Naturists.

ALISON Soft porn? You mean soft porn, Mum. That's what it's called, these days.

ELSPETH I thought that would be the worst –

ALISON There's no harm in that. Everybody watches soft porn. Nearly everyone we know does, anyway.

ELSPETH I don't. Do you watch it, with – Brian, then?

ALISON Now and then, when the kids have gone to bed. If we're feeling like a little extra something – you know –

ELSPETH What sort of extra something?

ALISON Just in order to get us started, you know – well to get him started really – I'm usually well up for it. But it's trickier for a man sometimes, you know. Specially if he's had a bad day at work, you know. Awkward clients –

ELSPETH Awkward clients? How do you mean, awkward clients?

ALISON Oh, for God's sake, Mum, he has trouble occasionally getting it up – that's all I mean!

A pause. She realises she may have upset her mother.

ELSPETH Oh, I see.

ALISON Sorry.

ELSPETH Maybe he could do with some of that Viagra, do you think?

ALISON No, Brian doesn't need Viagra, Mum. He's not that past it, for God's sake. He – he just needs to start coming home at regular times more often. Stop hanging around in the pub with his mates, till all hours... Nothing wrong with Brian. *(muttering to herself)* ...A few weeks on the wagon, wouldn't put right...no there's nothing wrong with Brian...

There is a silence between them. **ELSPETH** *studies her daughter, sensing they may have both taken a path that neither of them intended to go down.*

ELSPETH So. Come on, then! What's all this about your father? What's he been up to? Come on, tell me the worst.

ALISON I'd better start from the beginning.

ELSPETH Just as you like.

ALISON Right. Well, it's to do with Nigel.

ELSPETH Nigel? What's it got to do with Nigel? Where does your brother come into it, for goodness' sake?

ALISON You know that old computer Dad uses? It used to belong to Nigel, didn't it?

ELSPETH Yes, he left it behind when he moved out. Bought himself a new one, didn't he?

ALISON Yes, well, he just left it, you know, with Dad. Showed him how to use it, how to navigate, how to get online and so on. But Nigel, being Nigel, he also went and left all his personal stuff on it, you know, his passwords, his personal ID, all that stuff. To all intents and purposes, Dad took over where Nigel left off. Typical of Nigel. But then you expect that with him. He never thinks, does he? Dead casual. You can't altogether blame Dad – for...

She trails off.

ELSPETH Go on, go on, then. I'm listening.

ALISON Yes, well, just over a week ago. One evening, Nigel's alone in the house, all on his own. Denise was at her pre-natal class. So he's all alone – thank God he was, in some ways – you know what Denise is like, she'd have hit the bloody roof if she'd been there – she'd have gone spare...

She pauses again.

ELSPETH *(impatiently)* Yes, do go on, Alison, I'm listening –

ALISON Yes, anyway, this woman comes to the door. Nigel's never seen her before in his life, but she's all friendly and introduces herself and claims to know him and you know Nigel, he's hopeless. And though he's never clapped eyes on the woman before – he thinks, maybe he has done. He's thinking, maybe he's met her somewhere and he's just forgotten, you know, the way you can. Perhaps on holiday for instance. Anyway, she's that friendly and pleased to see him, the next thing is he invites her in. I mean, can you imagine him actually doing that? Inviting her into his home, a complete stranger? He's such a wally –

ELSPETH So he asks her in. And then?

ALISON Well he makes her a cup of tea and they're sitting there chatting away, or rather he says she was chatting away, he's just sitting there wondering where the hell he's met her before. But as she goes on, it becomes very clear that she isn't just someone he's casually met, she knows practically every single thing about him. His secret feelings, girls he fell in love with at school. A lot of his private thoughts, you know, his innermost...feelings, while he was growing up. Things she could never have normally known. No one could. Not possibly.

ELSPETH So what did he say to her?

ALISON Well, in so many words he said, "Sorry, I think you must be mistaken. You're obviously confusing me with someone else." And she said, "No, I haven't, you and I, we've been corresponding for weeks." And then she produces these letters she claims he'd written to her, typewritten letters. And he says to her, "I've never written a letter to you in my life, I don't even know where you live." And she says, "Just the far side of Birmingham and these aren't letters they're emails you've sent me." And then suddenly the penny drops. They were emails Dad had sent her. Dad had been carrying on an email correspondence with this poor woman for months on Nigel's old machine. All the time pretending to be Nigel, aged seventeen.

ELSPETH How did he manage that? To fool her? He's sharp enough with some things, your dad, but he's hardly known for his creative writing, is he?

ALISON Well, he managed to fool her. He'd based his letters on some of Nigel's. Ones he'd left in this file. Dad obviously found them.

ELSPETH What letters were these, then? Who was Nigel writing to?

ALISON Oh, this girl at school. Years ago. Mandy Westwick.

ELSPETH Mandy Westwick? Who the hell's Mandy Westwick, when she's at home?

ALISON She was in the sixth form with Nigel. He had a real thing about her. You must remember her. Mandy Westwick. Tall girl, ginger-haired, slightly knock-kneed.

ELSPETH Oh, her! Didn't she run away to London, then? With that bloke?

ALISON Yes, promised her an introduction to the fashion industry – fashion industry! Probably ended up sewing buttons on shirts. Never got onto the cover of *Vogue*, anyway. She did a runner overnight. Really upset her parents. Broke Nigel's heart, too. He had a real thing about Mandy Westwick.

ELSPETH Oh, I remember her now. Very dry skin, I recall.

ALISON Mad about her, was Nigel. He wrote her all these love letters, emails, apparently. Dozens of them. He told me he kept the whole correspondence, his and hers, in a secret file with its own secret password.

ELSPETH What was the password?

ALISON Mandy.

ELSPETH Brilliant! Who'd ever have guessed? He's a genius, my son.

ALISON Dad seemed to have no trouble opening it, anyway.

ELSPETH Why on earth did Nigel leave them on there in the first place for your father to find, if they were supposed to be secret?

ALISON Nigel said he'd forgotten all about them.

ELSPETH I thought he was mad about this girl?

ALISON Well, you know men. Out of sight, out of mind. A couple of months after Mandy left, he was off with Denise, wasn't he? Got engaged to her. You know what Nigel was like at that age. Flitting from one thing to the next. Never could settle, could he? Mind, he's calmer now. Since he's been married.

ELSPETH Yes, Denise has seen to that, hasn't she? So your dad managed to open this ever-so-special secret file, which Nigel had totally forgotten about, and then, pretending to be a teenager, he writes love letters based on Nigel's love letters to Mandy Westwick, to this woman from near Birmingham on the Internet who your dad's never even met and, as far as we know, he still hasn't met? The only person who's actually met her is Nigel who hadn't the faintest idea who she was in the first place? Have I got it roughly right so far?

ALISON That's the gist of it, Mum.

ELSPETH Well, I agree with you. Nigel's an idiot. And what's more it appears this woman's extremely stupid, too. How old is she, for God's sake, do we know? Did Nigel say?

ALISON I think she's about your age.

ELSPETH *My* age?

ALISON Maybe a year or two younger. So Nigel said.

ELSPETH Well, I've no sympathy for her, none at all, she's clearly half-witted as well. Old enough to know better. What on earth did she think she was doing, carrying on with a boy of eighteen? She should be ashamed of herself at her age.

ALISON She pretended she was seventeen.

ELSPETH She's as bad as him, then! My God, what were they playing at? Two grown people pretending to be teenagers! That is so sad, Alison! It's deeply, deeply sad!

ALISON Yes, it was. Once she realised, this woman was really upset. Sat there crying her eyes out for ages. Refused to leave. Nigel was terrified Denise would come home from her pre-natal classes. How was he going to explain a hysterical woman on their sofa? You can't blame her for being upset, can you? I think she'd been pinning her hopes on it –

ELSPETH What, having an affair with a teenage boy she'd never even met? In her dreams, love! No, I've no sympathy for her, now. I'm sorry, I think that's just pathetic. *(with a sudden smile)* Must have been funny, though, mustn't it? *(frowning)* No, seriously, Alison. How can you possibly feel sorry for someone like that? No really. *(smiling again)* I'd have paid good money to have been there, I really would. Poor Nigel.

She laughs.

ALISON *(laughing with her)* ...Sitting there while she was telling him all about himself. Privately thinking, "Who the hell is she? I can't have been that pissed surely?" Poor woman!

ELSPETH Stupid baggage!

ALISON Daft cow!

ELSPETH Serves her right! What happened to her in the end? I presume he got rid of her?

ALISON She left eventually. Just in time. Nearly ran into Denise in the road on her way out. Pretended she was collecting jumble for the church.

ELSPETH Lucky escape.

ALISON For Nigel. If she'd found out about it, Denise would have flattened him. Seven months pregnant or not.

ELSPETH Yes, she's got a temper on her has Denise, hasn't she? I did warn him, but he wouldn't listen to me. Never listens to his mother. Remember Denise at their wedding? Getting furious at that organist for playing the wrong music.

ALISON "You're supposed to be a professional musician, man! We're paying enough for you!" Mind, she was in the middle of her morning sickness, you have to make allowances.

ELSPETH Not a state to be in at your wedding, is it? Maybe that's why most weddings are in the afternoon.

They both laugh.

ALISON Well. We may have got rid of this woman, whoever she was, "Bashful from Birmingham." But what are we going to do about Dad? I mean, technically, he's guilty of identity theft, isn't he? Stealing someone's identity online. That's a crime.

ELSPETH No one's going to prosecute him for that, surely? Certainly not Nigel. He won't prosecute his own father. No, it'll all fizzle out of its own accord. If your dad writes to her again she certainly won't write back, not now.

ALISON What if he tries it again with someone else? He's still got Nigel's computer, hasn't he? What if he does it again? No, you'll have to tackle him about it, Mum, you really have to.

ELSPETH Maybe.

ALISON No, not maybe. You must.

ELSPETH It's odd, you know, thinking of him out there in his shed, carrying on an affair with another woman. It's an odd feeling. Here was I, thinking the worst he was up to was looking at a bit of soft porn.

ALISON Hardly an affair, though, was it?

ELSPETH It feels like it was.

ALISON They hadn't even met. Not face to face. They never touched each other.

ELSPETH I still think of it as being unfaithful. In a way. There are lots of ways of being unfaithful, you know. I never thought he'd be unfaithful. Not Arthur. Not to me. I know lots of women of my age, their husbands go off, chasing a younger model. Sometimes they come back, sometimes they don't. Depends how strong the roots are in their marriage. How deep they've grown. I never thought it would happen to me though. Silly. What's so special about me?

ALISON You're special, Mum. Very special. To all of us.

ELSPETH No, that's sweet of you to say, love, but I'm just another silly wife, that's all. Took my eye off the ball, didn't I?

ALISON Well, he's done the same to you, hasn't he? Look at him now, out there in his shed. Like he is every single bloody night. Never sits with you, does he? Hardly speaks to you, half of the time. Unless he wants something. When did you last go out together, Mum? For a meal? You and him? Go out to a movie? When did you both just sit down, the two of you, and watch telly together?

ELSPETH What, in that front room? We'd freeze to death before they got to the commercials.

ALISON No, honestly, Mum! Dad's neglected you just as badly. If not worse. He's the one's taken his eye off the ball, if anyone has.

ELSPETH I don't think we can blame him. It takes two, you know, Alison.

ALISON Don't know what you mean. Don't know why you keep insisting on taking the blame. Maybe you ought to, then?

ELSPETH What?

ALISON I said maybe you should. Have an affair of your own. After all, you're entitled.

ELSPETH No one's entitled to be unfaithful to someone they promised to love.

ALISON Very noble.

ELSPETH It's not noble, Alison. It's honourable. I don't think we've been honourable to each other. Either of us.

ARTHUR *is heard unlocking the back door as he returns.*

ALISON *(loudly)* So that's all settled then...

ELSPETH *(picking up on her)* Yes I think we've come to some sort of conclusion...

ALISON So you'll be saying something about it shortly, Mum?

ARTHUR *(closing the back door)* Saying what?

ELSPETH Oh, yes I'll be saying something, don't worry.

ALISON I mean it can't go on, can it? So long as you do say something.

ARTHUR What's she saying about what?

ELSPETH Alison, don't worry, leave it to me. You're to leave it to me!

ARTHUR What are you leaving to her?

ELSPETH I'll tell him.

ALISON If you're quite sure. All right?

ELSPETH All right.

ARTHUR *(loudly)* I say, you two, excuse me! I am here now, you know –!

ALISON *(kissing her mother)* See you soon, Mum. Take care.

ELSPETH *(embracing her)* You take care too, darling.

ARTHUR Hey! For your information, I've just entered the room, in case you hadn't noticed!

ELSPETH Love to Brian.

ALISON Oh, yes, he sends his to you. *(kissing* ARTHUR *fleetingly on the cheek)* Bye, Dad. See you later.

ARTHUR Oh, great, you have noticed me. That's a relief.

ALISON *(as she goes out)* See you in a day or two, then. Bye!

ELSPETH Bye!

ARTHUR Bye!

> ALISON *goes out.*

> What's up with her? Like I'm the bloody invisible man. Both of you. What's going on?

ELSPETH We were just discussing Christmas, that's all.

ARTHUR Christmas? Didn't sound like Christmas to me.

ELSPETH We were talking about Christmas. You know, what people wanted.

ARTHUR Ah, yes. Now. I've had an idea about that. Something I wanted –

ELSPETH Yes, you've already said. You want tokens –

ARTHUR – No, not tokens –

ELSPETH – You'll get your blessed tokens, it's all right, don't worry –

ARTHUR – No, not tokens, something else. I thought of something else I needed.

ELSPETH Something else?

ARTHUR Out there just now, while I was in the shed, I was thinking. What I really could do with – it's expensive, mark you – it won't come cheap –

ELSPETH How expensive?

ARTHUR It depends. Depends, on how much you're prepared to spend. Don't worry, if it's difficult, I'm willing to go halves –

ELSPETH What is it?

ARTHUR – It's not going to break the bank, don't worry –

ELSPETH Arthur, just tell me what it is.

ARTHUR A new computer. A new laptop. I need a new one.

ELSPETH (*faintly*) A new one?

ARTHUR Nigel's quite right. That one's completely clapped out. I've hung onto it far too long. It's over twenty years old. It's no longer fit for purpose.

ELSPETH I see.

ARTHUR I mean, it's totally clogged up. The memory's filled with all sorts of stuff – my stuff, Nigel's old stuff – I've tried deleting, tried getting rid of some of it – but frankly it's long past its sell-by date. It keeps crashing. No, I've made up my mind. Time for a new one. Time to move on.

ELSPETH *is silent.* ARTHUR *stares at her.*

What's the matter, then? We can afford it. What do you think?

ELSPETH Yes. I think it's a good idea. You're in need of a new one, aren't you?

ARTHUR I am.

ELSPETH That old one must be filled with all sorts of your rubbish.

ARTHUR Yes, I said.

ELSPETH All Nigel's old rubbish, as well. You're in need of a new one.

ARTHUR I could maybe look online, see if I can find one secondhand. You know, reconditioned –

ELSPETH No, not secondhand! That'll have someone else's old stuff on it, won't it? No, you need a brand-new one of your own. Start afresh.

ARTHUR If you're sure.

ELSPETH New memory. Nice clean screen. Clean everything.

ARTHUR Right.

ELSPETH Good. Then that's all settled. That's you taken care of, isn't it? That's a big relief.

A pause.

ARTHUR *stares at her, picking up something in her tone.*

ARTHUR – Er...

ELSPETH Yes?

ARTHUR Anything in particular you'd like, is there? From me? I mean, other than tokens. Anything special you fancy?

ELSPETH No, I'm happy to settle for tokens.

ARTHUR All right. If you're sure.

ELSPETH Mind you, this year, if you don't mind, I'd like them to be special tokens.

ARTHUR Special? How do you mean, special?

ELSPETH Oh, don't worry, they won't cost any more. In fact they'd be perfectly free. They'd be Time Tokens.

ARTHUR Time Tokens?

ELSPETH Tokens of your time. That I could spend as I wanted.

ARTHUR I don't think I'm quite following this? How do you get hold of them? Who issues these tokens?

ELSPETH You do. "I, Arthur, owe you, Elspeth, one hour of my time." Something like that. Quite simple. Doesn't need to be very complicated. You could run them off on your new computer. You can run some off for yourself as well, if you like.

ARTHUR What? "You..."?

ELSPETH "...I, Elspeth, owe you, Arthur..." You could run a few of those off too, while you're at it!

ARTHUR For me to use?

ELSPETH Yes.

ARTHUR Whenever I wanted?

ELSPETH Whenever you wanted.

ARTHUR What, even if you're off out somewhere?

ELSPETH Whenever.

ARTHUR Right. I'll run some of those off, too. How many do you reckon we need?

ELSPETH We'll see how it works first, shall we? We can always run off more if needs be, can't we?

ARTHUR I'll need a new printer.

ELSPETH After a time, we may not even need them. Maybe we could learn to trust each other again. Tell you what, we'll both go out first thing tomorrow, shall we, have a look round for a new laptop?

ARTHUR What, both of us together?

ELSPETH Why not? I'll use one of my tokens. I'll trust you. It's a long time since we both went shopping together, isn't it? Be nice. *(moving to the door)* Coming up, are you?

ARTHUR *(following her)* This shopping trip? You're not planning on going into any dress shops, are you?

ELSPETH *(as she goes out)* I might do. See how I feel...

ARTHUR *(as he goes out)* Bloody hell...

As they both go out, the lights fade to:

Blackout.

End of Play

PROPS

Drinks glasses

Pen

Crumpled notes

Reading glasses

Kitchen table

Dinner dishes and last stages of meal

Back-door key

Mobile phone

Handbag

SOUND EFFECTS

Knowing Her

Knowing Him

LIGHTING

Knowing Her

Knowing Him

ABOUT THE AUTHOR

Alan Ayckbourn has worked in theatre as a playwright and director for over fifty years, rarely if ever tempted by television or film, which perhaps explains why he continues to be so prolific. To date he has written more than eighty plays, many one-act plays and a large amount of work for the younger audience. His work has been translated into over thirty-five languages, is performed on stage and television throughout the world and has won countless awards.

Major successes include: *Relatively Speaking, How the Other Half Loves, Absurd Person Singular, Bedroom Farce, A Chorus of Disapproval,* and *The Norman Conquests.* In recent years, there have been revivals of *Season's Greetings* and *A Small Family Business* at the National Theatre; in the West End *Absent Friends, A Chorus of Disapproval, Relatively Speaking* and *How the Other Half Loves*; and at Chichester Festival Theatre, major revivals of *Way Upstream* in 2015 and *The Norman Conquests* in 2017. 2019 also saw the publication of his first work of prose fiction, *The Divide.*

Artistic director of the Stephen Joseph Theatre from 1972–2009, where almost all his plays have been first staged, he continues to direct his latest new work there. He was honoured to be appointed the SJT's first Director Emeritus during 2018. He has been inducted into the American Theater Hall of Fame, received the 2010 Critics' Circle Award for Services to the Arts and became the first British playwright to receive both Olivier and Tony Special Lifetime Achievement Awards. He was knighted in 1997 for services to the theatre.

Other plays by ALAN AYCKBOURN
published and licensed by Concord Theatricals

Absent Friends

Arrivals and Departures

Awaking Beauty

Bedroom Farce

Better Off Dead

Body Language

A Brief History of Women

Callisto 5

The Champion of Paribanou

A Chorus of Disapproval

Comic Potential

Communicating Doors

Consuming Passions

Confusions

A Cut in the Rates

Dreams from a Summer House

Drowning on Dry Land

Ernie's Incredible Illucinations

Family Circles

Family Circles

Farcicals

FlatSpin

GamePlan

Gizmo

Haunting Julia

Henceforward...

Hero's Welcome

House & Garden

How the Other Half Loves

If I Were You

Improbable Fiction

Intimate Exchanges, Volume I

Intimate Exchanges, Volume II

It Could Be Any One of Us

Joking Apart

Just Between Ourselves

Life and Beth

Life of Riley

Living Together